1000 LASHES

Foreword by Lawrence M. Krauss

RAIF BADAWI
1000 LASHES
BECAUSE I SAY WHAT I THINK

Edited by **CONSTANTIN SCHREIBER**
Translated by **AHMED DANNY RAMADAN**

GREYSTONE BOOKS
Vancouver/Berkeley

1000 Peitschenhiebe. Weil ich sage, was ich denke
© by Ullstein Buchverlag GmbH, Berlin. Published in 2015
by Ullstein Verlag

15 16 17 18 19   5 4 3 2 1

Greystone Books Ltd.
www.greystonebooks.com

Cataloguing data available from Library and Archives Canada
978-1-77164-209-5 (pbk.)
978-1-77164-210-1 (epub)

Editing by Constantin Schreiber
Copy editing by Shirarose Wilensky
Front cover design by Sabine Wimmer, Berlin
Interior and back cover design by Nayeli Jimenez
Cover photo courtesy of Ensaf Haidar
Printed and bound in Canada by Friesens
Distributed in the U.S. by Publishers Group West

We gratefully acknowledge the financial support of the Canada
Council for the Arts, the British Columbia Arts Council, the
Province of British Columbia through the Book Publishing Tax
Credit, and the Government of Canada through the Canada
Book Fund for our publishing activities.

Greystone Books is committed to reducing the consumption
of old-growth forests in the books it publishes. This book
is one step towards that goal.

TABLE OF CONTENTS

• • •

FOREWORD

• • •

I wanted to break the walls of ignorance...

RAIF BADAWI

"FREETHINKING" AND "Saudi Arabian" are two descriptors that rarely appear in the same sentence, and for good reason. The former is officially outlawed by the government and religious leaders associated with the latter. For this reason, it is difficult to get a real sense of the difficulties experienced by those who live in Saudi Arabia and who do not want to be shackled by the chains of myth, hatred, and ignorance that are the hallmark of religious fundamentalism.

Most freethinking young people choose to leave the country and work in a more enlightened environment, or if they choose to stay, they keep their views to themselves. One such individual did not: Raif Badawi. For that he was tried and convicted and originally sentenced to death, a sentence that was then reduced to ten years of imprisonment, one thousand lashes, and a fine of a million Saudi riyals.

I confess I learned only relatively recently about Raif Badawi, following an article in the *Guardian* about his sentence and the fact that he had received the first installment of fifty lashes. I was sufficiently horrified that I relayed the article in tweets and posts so that others could learn of this most recent affront to human dignity by a dictatorial regime that is portrayed in much of the Western media and by the U.S. government as a friend of the West.

Such is the power of propaganda in our society that the Saudi regime is portrayed as benign and friendly amid an otherwise violent and dangerous world in the Middle East. We read about ISIS, Iran, and Al-Qaeda but rarely about the violent medieval forms of justice meted out in our oil-rich ally.

By attempting to silence those who criticize the status quo in their country, the Saudi government obviously hopes to not only better control those within its borders but also the perception of that country as seen by those from outside. Thus, it is more important than ever that the words of Arab thinkers and writers who oppose the oppression in their country reach out beyond its borders.

After reading about Raif, I was led to examine the blogs for which he had been convicted. Far from being dogmatic and strident, as I had expected, they are often filled with irony and sarcasm. His blogs, largely composed in the period of 2010 to 2012, before his arrest, span a wide variety of topics, from his (premature, in retrospect) enthusiasm about the Arab Spring uprising then beginning in Egypt to his prescient worry about future attempts to establish an Islamic caliphate in the region. But the heart of his writing goes beyond considerations of politics elsewhere; it examines the hypocrisy, and the consequences of that hypocrisy, associated with the strictures imposed upon free and open discussion within Saudi Arabian society.

I was initially particularly taken by a sarcastic piece related to my own field of study, written after a television preacher in Saudi Arabia called for astronomers to be punished on the grounds that they encouraged skepticism about sharia law. In "Let's Lash Some Astronomers" (p. 8), Badawi exhorts, "Truthfully, I am paying full attention to these preachers. They are teaching us all about a fact that was hidden from us: There seems to be a science called the Sharia Astronomy that I wasn't aware of. What an interesting and beautiful concept that is. In my humble experience, and my dedicated research in the matters of the universe and its planets, I've never come across anything like it. I call upon NASA to abandon its telescopes and take advantage of our sharia astronomers. It seems to me their sight is sharper than those broken telescopes at NASA."

For statements such as this Raif was sentenced to death! What makes this particularly repugnant, at least to me, is that ridicule is of vital importance in a free society. No subject should be above ridicule. Nothing should be so sacred as to be protected from humor, for fear that humor might induce reflection, and reflection might induce questioning, and questioning might induce freethinking.

This is precisely why people like Raif Badawi must not be silenced. Theocracies, like the one in Saudi Arabia, rely on preserving ignorance and fear as way of maintaining control of people's minds and actions. Swords and bombs ultimately have only temporary impacts in changing circumstances. Once people's minds are opened, however, there is no going back. That is why Saudi Arabia risked the consternation of the outside world by imprisoning an otherwise harmless young man and subjecting him to torture and isolation.

And that is why we need to support Raif and others like him who are brave enough to stay within the borders of their homeland and use the weapons of their pens, computers, and voices to fight for freedom of thought, expression, and action. People sometimes thank me for being brave enough to speak out on various issues, but this is all done within a society where the most likely negative response is hate mail or angry tweets. But the kind of bravery exhibited by those who speak their minds in countries where doing so puts them at constant risk is true bravery that should be celebrated by all of us. Raif himself expressed concern about this very fact when he wrote in 2010: "I'm really worried that Arab thinkers will migrate in search of fresh air and to escape the sword of the religious authorities."

The writings in this volume are simple, sometimes naïve but always heartfelt and thoughtful. The prose is clear and provocative. They offer readers a window into the minds of all those young Saudi Arabians who yearn for their country to enter the twenty-first century. These young people are the hope for the future, and we need to support them and oppose those who oppress them.

These young people, like Raif, do not want to violently overthrow the Saudi regime. They want to offer an alternative that can drag their country into the future. They recognize that religious fundamentalism is holding millions of people back from economic prosperity, health, and safety. As Raif so poignantly put it, when urging the separation of church and state: "Secularism respects everyone and does not offend anyone ... Secularism ... is the practical solution to lift countries (including ours) out of the third world and into the first world."

Regardless of your views of religion and its place in the human condition, all those among us who are lucky enough to live in a society where we are free (albeit within the constraints of somewhat limited access to media largely dictated by those with wealth and power) to ridicule and criticize need to show solidarity with those, like Raif, who, because of an accident of birth, are less fortunate as they struggle for a better, freer world. We can do this by making sure writers like Raif are not silenced and the harsh but beautiful light of reality is allowed to shine on all of us.

LAWRENCE M. KRAUSS
Phoenix, Arizona

PREFACE

. . .

WE CAN ONLY marvel at Raif Badawi's courage. Why demonstrate when you live in a beautiful house, when you have enough food in the refrigerator, when you will be well taken care of in times of illness? Why push for political reform and jeopardize your job prospects? Why challenge the Islamic authorities when you are fully aware of the potential consequences—lashing, jail time, punitive fines? And all this for something that brings you no income, no house, no job—for no greater reason than to say and write what you think?

The Saudi blogger Raif Badawi has risked all and lost much for precisely that reason. He lost his freedom (ten years' imprisonment), his money (a fine of 1 million Saudi riyals, or more than one quarter of a million U.S. dollars), his family (his wife, Ensaf, had to flee with their three children to Canada). And on top of all this, he has to endure one thousand lashes, because, in his blog, he criticized the Saudi government and the power of Islamic scholars. Such action takes great courage and the conviction that one is changing things not only for oneself but also for society as a whole. The thirty-one-year-old was driven by a deep-seated fear that things were moving in absolutely the wrong direction.

Raif Badawi comes from the town of Khobar in eastern Saudi Arabia. The most formative experience in his youth was the early death of his mother, which deeply affected the whole family. After his schooling, he worked in a local business. He got to know his wife-to-be, Ensaf, through a chance encounter. One day, Raif dialed a wrong number and Ensaf answered. The two of them ended up speaking on the phone for a long time. Many more telephone conversations followed, without the pair ever having set eyes on each other. The first time Raif saw his wife-to-be was when she appeared in the window of her home. The two wanted to get married when they were still in their teens, but Ensaf's family was strictly opposed to the idea, because they felt their daughter was too young. In 2002, the couple prevailed and were finally able to marry. It was a love match, as both of them repeatedly emphasize. That is unusual in Saudi Arabia, where parents frequently arrange marriages. It could well be that the death of his mother and the fight for his personal happiness led Raif to develop a particular empathy for issues and people and for the world in which he lived.

Raif Badawi did not follow the path chosen by other young Arabs. He did not head for the West. He had the same motivations as they did to do so: young Saudis are fed up with being forced into lifestyles that have little to do with modernity. They want to say what they think, meet with whomever they want, dress as they wish. But few dare to fight and suffer for these desires—so they leave their homeland in the hands of those who want to make it more conservative, strict, and backward-looking.

There are many observers who say that the Arab world is now experiencing its Age of Enlightenment. Since the onset of the Arab Spring in 2011, the Middle East has supposedly found itself in a period of development similar to the one Europe went through three hundred years ago—as though it were in a time warp. Discussions are now taking place about the role of the state and religion. It is a struggle that brings both advances and retreats. Back in 2012, Boualem Sansal, the Algerian writer and winner of the Peace Prize of the German Book Trade, saw the European Enlightenment as a model for countries in the Arab world. Wrong, writes Badawi. There is no historical timeline, akin to a law of nature, that lays out a particular result from events according to a plan: first A, then B, then C. And so it makes little sense to simply transpose the European Age of Enlightenment onto Arab countries. Badawi does compare events in the Middle East with the French Revolution but comments that this shows there are no historical models for radical political changes. Indeed, this turning point in European history did not develop according to any known pattern. It was completely unclear what France would look like after the revolution or even how long its revolutionary period would last. So developments in the Arab world will unfold in their own ways, ways that will not take direction from earlier historical precedents and certainly not from those that have taken place in the West.

The discussion about the role of the state and religion in the Arab world is not new, but the Arab Spring has brought it to the forefront. As early as the end of the nineteenth century, a movement for reform in the Arab world was underway. The so-called al-Nahda—often translated as "renaissance"—fueled an identity crisis and led to an examination of the societal influences of religion and relationships with the West. More than a few Arab intellectuals at the time—for instance, the Syrian intellectual Farah Antun—were demanding non-religious forms of government. His writings, set down at the beginning of the twentieth century, exhibit astounding parallels with Badawi's texts, formulated one hundred years later. Antun, like Badawi, traced the backwardness of the Arab world to the belief system of Islam and pushed for secularization. The world wars and, finally, the leaden dictatorships in Egypt, Syria, Libya, and other countries brought a premature end to the school of thought championed by Antun and many other liberal thinkers.

The comparison Badawi draws with the French Revolution is, in its historical dimension, not too farfetched when it comes to the epic upheavals in the Middle East. Many Western governments were downright euphoric when a wave of change spread from Tunisia out across the Arab states. This wave toppled regimes and was supposed to usher in an age of democracy as we understand it. Whole peoples stood up and demanded to be heard. In 2011, U.S. president Barack Obama spoke of the "flame of hope" kindled by the Arab Spring and was, along with other politicians in the West, exhilarated by the prospect that democratic engagement along Western lines was to take up its natural place in the Middle East, because they thought it was superior. That was 2011.

In 2015, the Arab world presents a gruesome picture: terrorist troops of Islamic factions are gaining ground. Libya, Syria, Iraq, and Yemen are all states in the process of disintegration and count among the most dangerous and frightening tracts of land in the world. The barbaric videos of mass executions and mutilations that we journalists have to sift through are too unbearable for us to include in our reports, even after we have blurred the details. They are too awful to even describe here.

Badawi's final blog entries date from 2012, that is to say, before the terror of the Islamic State of Iraq and Syria (isis) descended on the region in full force. Since then, Badawi has sat in prison condemned to silence. But his posts, long extinguished by the Saudi authorities, are more relevant than ever. Consider, for example, Badawi's homeland, Saudi Arabia. On the one hand, the kingdom is a state that more than any other is attempting a social and political high-wire act, and it is not clear if it will succeed in the long run. On the other hand, the country's oil millionaires have promoted the country into the premier leagues of the richest states with the most up-to-date infrastructure and the best cellphone and Internet connections, which make it technically possible for its inhabitants to keep in contact with the modern world.

However, the kingdom, as the land that has within its borders both Mecca and Medina—Islam's two most important sites—is particularly bound by a conservative religious orientation. It sees within its technological capabilities a danger for the character of Islamic society; therefore, that technology must be opposed. With increasing modernity on one side and increasing Islamization on the other, tension in the country increases and the attempts to balance these opposing forces become more desperate. State censorship is a gigantic undertaking that continually searches the Internet for pornographic websites or websites that criticize the regime. Badawi writes: "The religious philosophy controlling our lives in Saudi Arabia is fighting a daily war to plant and impose the lines of Salafi religious ruling, which was forced upon us hundreds of years ago."

Naturally, in many of his writings, Badawi concerns himself primarily with Saudi Arabia, because he knows the social stratifications in his home best and in most detail—but again and again, he also analyzes the direction the Middle East as a whole is taking, not only politically, culturally, and socially but also economically. Take, for example, the Egyptian revolution in 2011. At first, the fall of longtime dictator Hosni Mubarak unleashed the hope that a new era of self-determination was about to break out in the country on the Nile. Even Badawi was among those swept up by the wave of euphoria that followed Mubarak's fall from power. Cairo, known to Arabs as *Umm al-Dunya*, or "the mother of the world," is the traditional cultural and political center of the Arab world. Like many others at the time, Badawi could not imagine this city would be plagued by unrest and bombings. Those who visit this metropolis of 20 million today notice the massive presence of security forces and the tense atmosphere in the country.

Increasing Islamization was difficult for many to imagine. In the past hundred years, the social makeup of Egypt, the largest Arab nation, has hardened from a melting pot of different religions and cultures into a clearly Islamic-oriented society in which minorities and those with other belief systems no longer have a place. As recently as the twentieth century, hundreds of thousands of Greeks lived in Egypt, and they played an important role in the economic and cultural life of the country. The city of Alexandria was, since its inception, a center for Hellenistic culture and home to progressive thinkers. Ten percent of Egyptians are Christians, and members of the Coptic Orthodox Church of Alexandria consider themselves to be the original Christians, because they were among the first to adopt the religion. Today, with the exception of a tiny minority in Alexandria, all Greeks have left the country. Some Coptic Christians in Cairo wear Muslim head coverings, because they would otherwise be pestered or would feel uncomfortable; many can no longer bear to live in Egypt and have left the country in which their forebears lived for almost two thousand years. Egypt continues to battle chaos. When Raif Badawi wrote his blog entries about the political situation in Egypt, at the time of the demonstrations in Tahrir Square, he could not have envisioned such a scenario.

But, as though he had foreseen what was coming, as early as 2010, Badawi warned against extremists who wanted to establish a new caliphate. From today's perspective, this writing seems downright prophetic. A few years later, the Islamic State terrorist organization did indeed follow through with the delusional idea of establishing an Islamic caliphate in Syria.

A further idea that Badawi explored is the concern that young people in the Arab world thirsty for knowledge would be forced by the theocracy to leave their homes. The result: states and societies in the Middle East are losing their connection with developing modernization and globalization.

Raif Badawi wrote his blogs at a critical time. In Syria and Iraq, Islamists are trying to bomb the region back into the darkness of prehistory. In other parts of the Arab world, governments are trying to hold onto the status quo any way they can, hoping to pull off the balancing act between traditional Islamic society and the possibility of modern life.

But Badawi's writings are also of great importance for us in the West. Muslim communities in Europe are caught up in the cultural and religious tensions between their backgrounds and those of the people around them. The discussion that Badawi leads is crucial for the Muslims among us. It is a reminder that progress and prosperity depend on plurality and tolerance. In times when Islamic extremists in Europe carry out attacks on employees of *Charlie Hebdo,* Badawi's writings are hugely relevant.

Raif Badawi has a clear belief system. He is an advocate for "liberalism"—a term he uses over and over again in his posts. "Live and let live" is the principle he abides by. The anger, the rage in the face of the suffocating straitjacket of Saudi society occasionally breaks through, as when he writes: "Any religion-based state has a mission to limit the minds of its people, to fight the developments of history and logic, and to dumb down its citizens." It is because of posts such as this that he has suffered severe punishment in Saudi Arabia and perhaps has even worse awaiting him.

It gives us all hope that in the midst of one of the most conservative countries in the world a young man can have such free thoughts and put himself in the way of danger because of these thoughts. It gives us all hope that young Muslims talk about how we can live together peacefully in a world in which religion has a firm place, but the opinions of individuals also count.

CONSTANTIN SCHREIBER
March 2015

EDITOR'S NOTE

•   •   •

UNFORTUNATELY, RAIF BADAWI'S posts, which are banned in Saudi Arabia, cannot be retrieved in their entirety. From those reconstructed with the help of his wife, Ensaf Haidar, we have chosen fifteen for publication in this book. The majority appeared between 2010 and 2012 in the online publications *Al-Bilad,* al-Hewar al-Mutamaddin, and Al Jazeera. It is impossible to pinpoint the online publication date for four of the chosen posts.

INTRODUCTION

．．．

I WAS ENGROSSED IN my attempts to reexamine liberalism in Saudi Arabia, which was contributing to the prevalence of "enlightenment" in my community. I wanted to break the walls of ignorance, to shatter the sacredness of religious clerics. I wanted to advocate for change and respect for freedom of speech, to call for women and minorities' rights, and the rights of the indigent in Saudi Arabia.

That was before I was jailed in 2012.

Imagine living your daily life, enacting all of its details, in a small 215 square-foot room, accompanied by more than thirty people accused of a variety of criminal activities. In prison, I socialized with people confined for criminal offenses: killers, thieves, drug lords, and pedophiles. My interactions with them altered many of my faulty understandings in regard to the world of criminals.

Before my imprisonment, like any other person, I would go to bed after I checked all the windows and doors in my home, for fear of criminals. Now, I lived among them; I slept, ate, showered, changed my clothes, celebrated and cried, got angry, laughed out loud, and screamed my lungs out... all while surrounded by their leering eyes.

After colossal effort and countless attempts to acclimate myself to them, I focused on changing my way of seeing them. I pulled the curtain from the other side and started to explore the depths of their world. It took me a while, but I came to the conclusion that criminals laugh, too. Yes, they fall in love, feel pain, and are capable of deep, soft human emotions. It is agonizing for me to compare those genuine feelings I witnessed with the negative perceptions of people I considered close to me in the past.

In the prison lavatory, I took a look around me, only to find some filthy tissues and excrement everywhere. It was a staggering situation: the walls were soiled; the doors were rusty and rotten. Here I was, trying to adapt to this new chaos. My eyes scanned the walls around me, reading the hundreds of sentences written on the sticky walls. My eyes caught an unexpected sentence: "Secularism is the Solution!"

I rubbed my eyes with both palms. For a second, I didn't believe what I was seeing. I wanted to be sure I was indeed reading what my eyes were locked upon. I escaped my reality for a second. I felt like I was standing in the middle of a dirty old nightclub in a poor neighborhood. By the wee hours of the night, a beautiful, mesmerizing woman walks in; she fills the nightclub with a stunning joy and life energy.

I hardly knew what made me think of that. Why was I pulled into this fantasy? It seems the change of toilet seat played a major role in the way I made sense of the new, strange life I was living.

I smiled. I wondered who the person might be who wrote such a sentence, in a prison filled to the walls with thousands of prisoners, all jailed because of criminal activities. My astonishment was equal only to my happiness at reading such a short, beautiful, and different sentence. The sentence stood alone among dozens of obscenities that were written in so many different Arabic dialects.

This discovery could only mean one thing. There was at least one other person here who understood me, who understood the reasons I was jailed and the goals I was hoping to accomplish.

In the following days, I started to see a whole different reality that turned this world of criminals into my own personal paradise. I built that heaven according to my own standards; I detailed it according to a new set of beliefs that departed from all my previous life experiences before my imprisonment.

Yes. Lavatory cell number five really touched me!

When my dear wife, Ensaf, told me a large publishing house in Germany was interested in collecting my articles in a book translated into German, I hesitated. I will be completely honest with you: when I wrote my first article, I couldn't imagine it would be gathered in a book in Arabic, let alone translated into a different language.

Well, if you picked up this book, managed to read this far, and you're still going, I can safely assume that you—my dear reader—are interested in reading what I have to say.

Some think I have something to say; others think I am an ordinary man with nothing to share, a man who doesn't deserve his writings to be collected in books or translated for the world to share. However, when I look within, I only see that thin man who miraculously withstood fifty lashes, while a group of people celebrated his pain, repeatedly chanting *Allahu Akbar.*

All for the articles you're about to read.

Yes. I was accused of apostasy (the conscious abandonment of Islam) and sentenced to death. The sentence was then reduced to ten years of imprisonment as well as one thousand lashes. I was also required to pay a million Saudi riyals in financial punishment.

I spent three years writing these articles for you: I was tortured; my wife and our three children had to emigrate from our country because of the many pressures placed upon them. My family and I endured all those harsh struggles simply because I spoke my mind. We went through these hardships for the sake of every letter written in this book.

1

Religious Vocation Entraps
the Freedom of the Arab Thinker

. . .

FREEDOM OF SPEECH is the air that any thinker breathes; it's the fuel that ignites the fire of an intellectual's thoughts.

Throughout the past centuries, nations and societies advanced through the work of their intellectuals, who present their ideas and philosophies. The people, thereafter, can pick from that pool of viewpoints whichever intellectual style suits them; they can even develop it to reach the deep seas of knowledge, progress, civilization, and prosperity.

Many civilizations and human rights organizations believe that freedom of speech is a basic human right, and they call upon the Arab regimes to reform their policies when it comes to freedom of speech. As a human being, you have the right to express yourself. You have the right to journey wherever your mind wanders and to express the thoughts you come up with along the way. You have the right to believe, and to atone, the same way you have the right to love and to hate. You have the right to be a liberal, or to be an Islamist.

Actually, all monotheistic religions insist on freedom of speech.

Let's take Islam, for example: there is a verse in the Quran that says, "And say, 'The truth is from your Lord, so whoever wills—let him believe; and whoever wills—let him disbelieve.'"

The meaning behind this verse needs no illumination; it is as clear as the light of the sun.

Arab thinkers, especially those who are blessed with a freethinking mind, are used to writing between the lines and dancing with their words around such topics. It is the only way for them to pass on their philosophy, particularly because those who present an enlightening rationale are considered blasphemous and atheist. The Arab societies are programmed to consider any freethinking idea to be a moral degradation. They consider it to be an act against religion and a departure from the righteous road.

Is this normal? Surely it isn't. Both sides—the Arab thinker and their society—are acting against their very nature. On the one hand, the thinker needs to unveil their ideas and philosophies on all matters clearly and courageously, even if their ideas are faulty, or if they stand against the status quo (in other words, the religion-inspired state of affairs).

On the other hand, the society needs to open its collective mind to all ideas and ideologies. It needs to give its people the chance to listen to the opinions of others, and then examine them critically instead of rejecting them prematurely. Such a creative dialogue based on positive critical thinking can enhance and develop ideas.

Observers of the Arab society easily identify the problem: the society is whimpering under the pressure of theocratic regimes that only tolerate murmurs of obedience from their people in response to their religious scholars.

Without a doubt, this society has mastered the art of religious allegiance to the clergy. The scholars' fatwas[1] and their explanations of what a religion means, are considered the absolute truth; they are considered holy. If a freethinker dares to embark on a journey on the seas of the holy and forbidden, they are faced with hundreds of fatwas released by the clergy. Those scholars threaten the rationalists and renounce them; they consider them apostates.

My biggest fear is that the enlightened Arab thinkers are going to leave the Arab world in search of fresh air: somewhere far away from the swords of the religious authorities.

2

Defaming the Intellectuals and the Inquisition Courts:
Turki al-Hamad as an Example

. . .

MANY OF THE Islamist activists of Saudi Arabia dream of the return of an era long gone: they fantasize about the times of the Abbasid caliph al-Mahdi or the Umayyad caliphs al-Mamun and al-Motawakel, among others. Those caliphs were known to banish and murder their opponents. They used defamation and accusations of apostasy, and they justified their actions under the ruling of a political Islam.

The modern Islamists hope history will repeat itself; and no one denies them their right to a dream. However, their actions have expanded beyond the limits of dreaming, turning into a well-organized advocacy system. They present their own vision of religion and faith, oppressing the public with their crooked views. Recently, they went as far as to compete with and challenge others over who is more in favor with the prophet, peace be upon him.

Yes, this is taking place right now, in the twenty-first century.

Many rejected Hamza's[2] messages on Twitter; they didn't wait for the official sentencing before judging him. The tweets of those calling for his blood were written by thirsty vampires.

Some of Hamza's detractors reached new lows when they linked his tweets with the Enlightenment movement as a whole. They went looking, with their sharp mouths and their heavy souls, for an ugly war against all who fight for civilization and enlightenment. They fight because they see the Enlightenment lobby as an offensive, anti-religion, apostate movement.

The extremist Islamist movement is working tirelessly to associate Kashgari with the Liberal movement. They present him to their followers as one of the most important liberalists in the country, which can't be any further from the truth. Kashgari is well known to be closer to the Muslim Brotherhood in Saudi Arabia; we never heard him acknowledge liberalism, let alone announce himself as a supporter.

The persecution of Kashgari is a failed and pathetic attempt by the extremists to find a loophole in the Law of Printed Material and Publications, which was promulgated by a royal decree. They wish to prosecute every writer and freethinker who doesn't echo their affirmations. They want to judge Kashgari under the laws of sharia that support their own ideologies, not the current laws, made possible by a royal decree.

The campaign against freedom of speech began in 1998, when writer Turki al-Hamad[3] was accused of apostasy. The extremists went after him and called for his head.

The most important question: What did al-Hamad say to cause that invasive, hostile reaction? He wrote in his novel a single sentence: "God and the Devil are two faces on the same coin."

Al-Hamad explained himself multiple times, in many an interview: a character in his novel, not al-Hamad himself, said this problematic sentence. Religiously speaking, the messenger is not responsible for the message he carries, according to Sheikh Mohammed bin Othman.[4] Grammatically speaking, the sentence is clear; it means that God and the Devil never meet; God in His glory takes the road of goodness, while the Devil aims for the road of evil. They are two faces that will never gaze into each other's the eyes, or take the same road, or look in the same direction.

Hashim, the character who said that sentence in the novel, was emotionally defeated; his mind wandered to such thoughts. At the time, decision-makers were able to see that, and they wisely ended the stream of fatwas against al-Hamad, officially terminating the crisis.

Nevertheless, the Islamist movement never rested.

For fourteen years, the Islamist movement continued to falsely portray al-Hamad to the public as a dangerous man and accused him of blasphemy and unbelief. Their only evidence was a sentence said by a character in a book, taken out of context and stripped of its indications.

To publicly defame al-Hamad, his enemies uploaded a tampered video of him to YouTube. The video was edited to single out that controversial sentence and omit the author's explanation. His enemies were successful in fooling many, who believed the doctored video.

I remember attending a Q&A event with al-Hamad in Jeddah's literature club, and when it was time for the audience's questions, an old man approached the stage. "I don't know that person," he said. "Thanks to Allah, I haven't read a single line he wrote. I heard he said a sentence against Allah, and I'm here to stand in this man's face for the sake of Allah," he continued.

This old man was but one of the many simple people who were emotionally manipulated by those who falsify facts and exploit the public.

3

Let's Lash Some Astronomers

. . .

ONE OF THE entertaining Islamic preachers is demanding that astronomers[5] face the consequences of their actions. "We are plagued with stargazers in recent years," the cleric says, "they are faulting the sharia vision." The Islamic scholars claim they are not against the science of astronomy. "It's a long-lived science," they add, "but we reject those who question the sharia vision." It seems the preachers consider those astronomers to be merely amateurs and youngsters, who have no right to stand in the face of sharia experts. They have been stargazing for the past thirty years.

Truthfully, I am paying full attention to these preachers. They are teaching us all about a fact that was hidden from us: There seems to be a science called the Sharia Astronomy that I wasn't aware of. What an interesting and beautiful concept that is. In my humble experience, and my dedicated research in the matters of the universe and its planets, I've never come across anything like it. I call upon NASA to abandon its telescopes and take advantage of our sharia astronomers. It seems to me their sight is sharper than those broken telescopes at NASA.

I believe NASA should send some of its scientists to our preachers to study real science. NASA's folks would be students sitting on their knees in the great classrooms of our sharia astronomers. I call upon all the scientists in the world in all different fields to abandon their offices and their labs, and leave behind their research centers and their universities, and to immediately join the circles of knowledge headed by our glorious preachers. Let the scientists of the world learn from our sharia scientists all kinds of modern knowledge: in medicine, engineering, chemistry, and geology. They should learn all about physics and nuclear science. They should learn all about oceanography, pharmacy, biology, and anthropology.

Don't forget, they should also learn about astronomy and space. You see, our preachers—may they live long and prosper—have proven they have the final word in everything. All humans should give up and surrender their minds to them without hesitation or questioning.

All the countries around the world are attracting all kinds of scientists; they offer them financial rewards and provide them with all kinds of technical and logistical support. These countries proudly grant nationalities to those scientists and help them undertake all the challenges in their search for knowledge and development.

We, on the other hand, sentence those who drink alcohol to eighty lashes. I wonder how many lashes those astronomers deserve...

4

No to Building a Mosque in New York City

. . .

O N SEPTEMBER 11, we remember the painful day of a terrorist attack that resulted in the deaths of more than three thousand people in New York City.

Coinciding with that painful memory, many Muslims in New York are calling for an Islamic center, including a mosque and a social lounge, to be built in the same area where the World Trade Center stood tall, before it trembled and fell upon the heads of those who died on that terrible day.[6]

What pains me most, as a citizen of the country that exported those terrorists (whom I'm naturally dishonored by), is the boldness of New York's Muslims, who did not think about the thousands of people who died on that dark day and their families. This brashness has reached the limits of insolence.

What bothers me even more is this chauvinist Islamist arrogance they display; they disregard the innocent blood spilled because of the plans of barbaric and brutal masterminds under the slogan of "*Allahu Akabar*."[7] They see this innocent blood as nothing compared with building a mosque that will undoubtedly hatch new terrorists. Not to mention, demanding to build such a mosque in such a location is a clear challenge to the American collective memory, as well as to humanity's collective memory. The human race as a whole rejects that scene of mass murder.

The question I must ask, as a global citizen first and a citizen of the country that originated those terrorists, is very simple: Why the arrogance? What kind of racist discrimination against innocent human blood allows us to demand such a thing?

Let's put ourselves in the shoes of the ordinary American: How open-minded are we going to be if a Christian or a Jewish person attacks us in our very home? Will we build a church or a synagogue for them in the same location as the attack? I highly doubt that.

We in Saudi Arabia refuse to build churches altogether. What do you think we would do if those who wanted to build such houses of worship were the same people who stormed our lands?

September 11 is a clear attack on the lands of a nation; the American nation as a whole was attacked.

Shouldn't we ask ourselves how come the United States allows Islamic missionaries to be active in its lands; and how come we never allow any missionaries to work in the lands of the Kingdom of Saudi Arabia? We cannot hide our heads in the sand from such questions anymore; we cannot pretend that no one hears us and that we care about no one. Like it or not, we're part of the human race, and we share the same duties and deserve the same rights as the rest of humanity.

The same way others respect our differences, we should respect the differences of others. Based on this great humanitarian concept, Custodian of the Two Holy Mosques King Abdullah bin Abdulaziz started his famous and great initiative Dialogue Between Religions,[8] hoping to gather us all under the one umbrella of human civilization. I'm not surprised to see the welcoming vibe the king's initiative has received from the whole world. King Abdullah bin Abdulaziz is a great leader and an international example; only through our intelligence can we keep up with the ever-developing world.

To respect the opinions of those who stand against you is nothing short of courageous. We need to be champions in accepting the beliefs of others and their right to make their own decisions and to believe in their own religions. That's why it's very important to realize how faulty it is when a group from within us demands a mosque be built in a location that is a heavy burden in the memories of Americans and all honorable people across the world.

The demographic and social structure of the United States respects the beliefs, religious values, and houses of worship of others, Abrahamic religions[9] or otherwise. This should be a calling for us to respect and appreciate the feelings of the victims' families and to say proudly and courageously: no to building a mosque in that very location. The free land of the United States is large and wide and accepts us all; it's possible to build this mosque elsewhere.

Finally, it's clear to observers that our Muslims in Saudi Arabia disrespect the beliefs of others. We consider them apostates. Those who are Muslims but are not believers in the Hanbali school[10] are seen, in a very limiting way, as aliens. Having this mentality in our society is destructive: How will we be able to build a human civilization with positive relations with the 7 billion people around the world when 5.5 billion of them don't even believe in Islam?

5

Yes! I Will Fight Theists and Religious Thoughts

. . .

I HAVE A FRIEND who is originally from one of the Levant countries.[11] He asked me once what my reaction would be if Hamas ever managed to liberate Palestine. I didn't hesitate. I told him I'd be the first person to stand and fight Hamas then.

My friend was shocked by my answer. "You would fight Hamas if it liberated Palestine?" he asked.

"Yes, even if it managed to wipe Israel off the face of the earth," I told him. "I'm sure it will never do so, but even if it did: I would be the first in line to fight it."

A moment of silence followed as I calmly finished my answer.

I'm against Israeli occupation of any Arab state, but I'm also against replacing Israel with a religious entity built on its ruins. Such a state would only seek to spread a culture of ignorance and death within its people. Instead, we need those who call for life and civilization. We need those who believe in planting hope in our souls.

Look at all the countries that are based on a religious ideology; look at their people and the generations born into it: What do they have to offer human civilization?

They offer nothing more than an irrational fear of a deity and an inability to challenge life.

These ideals continue to lead the way for generations to come: those generations are incapable of creative thought, incapable of building culture. They are unable to create their own modern structure or even practice the systems of civilization bestowed upon them by others.

Any religion-based state has a mission to limit the minds of its people, to fight the developments of history and logic, and to dumb down its citizens. It's important to stand in the way of such a mentality, to deny it from continuing its mission to murder the souls of its people, killing them deep within while they are still alive and breathing.

What we need the most in our Arab and Islamic societies is to realize the importance of the individual and the value of individualism. We need to appreciate the person, value their freedoms, and respect their intelligence.

Back in the medieval ages, European societies were under the tight control of the priesthood.

They used to interfere with every small detail of the people's daily life. Thus, ignorance and darkness prevailed, and wealth was common among those clerics. The priests worked tirelessly day and night to support and benefit from the ignorance. One of their techniques to control people was to sell them indulgences, promising them salvation from eternal damnation.

So, how do you expect me not to fight such doctrinal thinking?

Look what happened after the European nations managed to remove those clergy from public life and limit them to their churches, denying them any role outside their walls. European countries developed into nations buzzing with civilization, active in building the rights of the individual and exporting knowledge and science to the rest of humanity. These communities welcomed the culture of enlightenment, life, and creativity as they led a revolution against ignorance in all its aspects.

Conversely, the religious philosophy controlling our lives in Saudi Arabia is fighting a daily war to plant and impose the lines of Salafi religious ruling, which was forced upon us hundreds of years ago. It doesn't take into account all the changes and the renaissance the world is going through. Isn't it illogical to now subscribe to such backward thinking?

States that are built on a religious foundation limit their own people in a circle of faith and fear. Abdullah al-Qasemi,[12] the chief proponent of logical thinking in the Arab world, agrees that other states celebrate the pleasures of brilliance, creativity, civilization, and life that are forbidden us.

We need to start working right now on rewriting our history on our own, away from the control of the theists in our lives. We need to rebuild our culture and our consciousness from the very beginning and open a new horizon to our future. Or else we will continue to put our tails between our legs for eternity; we will be condemned to our unacceptable ignorance, while the rest of the civilized world enjoys a life full of hope in a better future. They export goodness to the rest of the world; when will we wake up to that?

6

Tahrir Square Brought Students Back to Hard Work

. . .

GYPT IS GOING through labor nowadays. It's not just a difficult delivery following a thirty-year fascist ruling that controlled the fate of the country and the dreams of its people, a ruling that killed the spirit of hope and advancement in the country, that killed the beauty of its song and dance.

What Egypt is going through right now is a challenge led by its students: the knowledge-seekers and the children of the bottom of the city. It's a revolution in all of its aspects, a decisive breakthrough not only in the history and geography of Egypt but also in all the Arab states controlled by autocrat dictatorships.

The January 25[13] revolutionaries started in Tahrir Square, which they turned into their own platform that knows no ceiling. They demanded the fall of the political tyranny ruling the country: a dictatorship led by a security-obsessed mentality.

That regime kept its distance from the tragic reality of its people. Egyptians were suffering daily to secure a loaf of bread (and not by bread alone does a man live), so they demanded a simple, dignified life, the same as all other people living in civilized nations.

Like a tourist, the Egyptian regime lived in Egypt for more than three decades with little knowledge of the situation of its people. The regime only cared to know the increasing number of its civilians. That regime had no worries. The reports placed every day on the president's desk, delivered by the intelligence services, confirmed a simple reality: the people are in a deep coma and the security situation is sustained.

It never crossed the collective mind of the Egyptian regime that the people, exhausted by hunger, would turn January 25, 2011, into something completely different from any other ordinary day. It never occurred to the regime that this date would change the map of its thirty-year-long delusional stability under the ruling of Hosni Mubarak, the same way an overpowering stream can dredge up everything in its channel.

In a few days, and with minimum losses, the activists at Tahrir Square managed to stand in the face of the security forces. Those carrying nightsticks never imagined such a day of change would come, a day that would alter their history of oppression and abuse.

The people of Egypt's neighboring countries were shocked when a few hundred young Egyptians shook the ground under the country's rulers and snatched continuous victories.

January 25 has proven that change is not impossible. The revolutionaries of Tahrir Square uncovered the truth: the will of the people is unbreakable, especially when there is a big gap between the desires of the ruling regime and of the people. The January 25 Revolution in Egypt examined the depth of the crisis facing regimes that were built upon intelligence reports and cared nothing for their struggling people.

So far, it's clear to us that Egypt is embracing its change. We have hope for a new dawn and a new Egypt. It will be born out of the womb of the suffering of its people and its students. Those revolutionaries took Tahrir Square and turned it into a theatre for a great historical event. The chants of the free were heard across Tahrir Square, signaling the end of an era of cowardliness, an era established through years of darkness by a worn-out regime.

I salute you, oh proud people who woke up from a long nap! I salute Tahrir Square, which welcomed the sons and daughters of Egypt on its grass, turning into a hostel for all of them, as the revolutionaries like to joke.

It's a hostel of freedom, not one for a dance and a song. But let's all sing together Sheikh Imam's[14] masterpiece: "The students are back to hard work. Egypt you will stay; you're the land of hopes and wishes."

7

The Traveler's Marriage and the Borrowed Ram

. . .

THE NAMES AND types of marriage contracts are many: some of them are permissible in sharia but rejected by tradition and logic. Such a tragedy is al-Misyar marriage: literally, the traveler's marriage.

Truthfully, al-Misyar should be named with its real purpose: a sexual encounter that takes away the rights of the woman.

It's a marriage between a man and a consenting woman, witnessed by people and attended by the woman's guardian. The contract states that the woman has to give up all her financial rights: her right to housing and her right to the monthly payment to cover her needs and the needs of her children should she get pregnant. She has to give up other religion-based rights, such as her right to equal treatment between her and the man's other wives.

She has to accept that her role is for the man to visit her chambers whenever it pleases him. Whenever he feels like enjoying a night of lovemaking, he "travels" to this fake wife, who is only his on paper, to spend a night comparable to the fantastical 1,001 nights. He is protected by religion and a binding legal contract.

This husband travels to his wife in his spare time; he stays with her for mere hours. He answers his passing whim and discharges his hidden needs. Then he goes back to where he came from, ending his fake role as her husband at her bedroom door.

While we're at it, let's discuss another animalistic marriage. It's a scene from another play! A man, considered a borrowed ram, spends one night with a borrowed wife, and then divorces her. You see, the purpose is to legally allow the woman to remarry her first husband: she was married to another man who divorced her, but they cannot get back together until she is legally married to another man and divorced once more. This borrowed ram opens the door for the first husband to remarry his divorced wife.[15]

It's a wonder of human behavior: we build our own handcuffs that trap and harm us. We create the myth, and we honor it. We tell the lie, and we believe it. We create a marriage contract, and then consider it permissible.

The names of marriage contracts are many, but death and obscenity remain one.

8

The Kingdom Come of
the Syrian Spring

. . .

"HERE I AM, once again, strangled between heaven and earth, flying solo in the abyss of a horizon, open only to my torturous questions."

To read this sentence as the opening to a novel, then find it waiting for you as the last line, means only one thing: you have lived a journey that you wish is over at the same time you wish to see it start again. It means you have lived the experience of exile within you and enjoyed reading about the experience of another, who is living their exile within your soul.

It means you have lived the experience of a novel that enlightened you with questions, as much as it provided you with answers. It means you went on a quest to find this experience in the land of reality, and you found it in the hottest spot on the planet now: the Syrian Spring, which we witnessed moving along since the 1980s.

That Syrian Spring exploded into one of the most burning revolutions in 2011, followed by disagreements among the leaders of the Syrian revolution. The only real name you'll find in the book is that of the opposition prisoner Riad al-Turk, who continues to be a legend of resistance. He resists the extinction of his own people not only in the pages of the novel but also on the streets of the resistance: he gathers, fights, and plants the seeds of hope that will soon bloom across the protests in the cities of Syria, patiently waiting under the fire of death.

The Queen of Kingdom Come, a novel published by the Arabian Institute for Studies and Publications at the end of 2006, by Syrian poet al-Muthanna al-Sheikh Attieh, is at its very core a story of an impossible love, the first challenge between the broken cosmic female and the forceful male. It tells the devastating psychological effects that such a clash would create within both the man and the woman: a deep, piercing exile. On the surface, it's a political novel about outcasts: the story of love that takes place under the shadows of persecution, imprisonment, and death at the hands of a dictatorship. The characters in the book have to make impossible choices in the days of a destructive war.

It seems that the harmony between the realistic side of the novel, its familiar characters, and the mythical, unfamiliar side of it, as well as the sensitive topics it tackles, is the reason it was banned in many countries. This is what makes *The Queen of Kingdom Come* a problematic novel on all levels, especially on the mythological and social levels, as well as on personal and universal levels, and on the levels of poetry and creative writing, in art, culture, literature, language, and structure.

It seems that this novel is driven insane by the death of memories in its 320 pages, holding its balance on the thin line of impossibilities, forcing its characters, as well as its readers, to walk the same line.

On the realistic and mythological levels, we see the issue of the greatest mother, Ishtar herself, represented in Noura, the sweet, loving girl who picked her man, gave him a child, and spread the soul of evergreen around her. She turns into a warrior facing the masculine ideologies that are challenging women. The story of the war continues in her son, who sees the destruction of the love affair between his mother and his father as a psychological disability that he attempts to overcome by immersing himself in the cosmic world of feminism, and in his fight for democracy, his support for feminist movements, and by fixing himself, through fixing others.

On the personal and universal levels, many discovered that the setting of the novel, its developments, and its characters are reflective of the biography of the writer himself: in his political work in Damascus, in his exile in Paris, and in his journalism work in *Shahrazad* magazine during the Second Gulf War. In his own words, the writer responds to that point, saying: "To consider me the real hero of my own book is something that strikes my ego: I will use it to attract the flocks of female fans who are in love with my main character, Hannibal al-Abad, but sadly, I'm not the main character, and al-Abad is a mixture of all of the characters of my friends and my colleagues, all of which are amazing at their work in the Syrian National Democratic opposition. I'm very proud of their friendship, and I'm thankful for my time with them."

On the poetry and creative writing front, Nadim Jarjourah, a famous critic, points out the poet's move to the art of writing novels, saying: "The novel is not just a representation of creative writing, nor is it a memoir of the author. It dips within one's soul and explores feelings and emotions, opening a wider door to more literature studies in his tangled worlds and questions. While moving from poetry writing to novel writing is the new trend in the Arab world, within the Arab cultural scene, this novel stands out in a beautiful way and stays true to its poetry origins, especially in its emotionally driven moments."

The novel is designed in an open structure, with two timelines of storytelling: the time of current reality, and the time of childhood. They work together in harmony at the beginning; then they interact and intertwine to the point of clear similarity. The structure clearly states the fates of its characters but also turns the end of the book upon its own beginning in a special way in which storytelling is also intertwining with poetry, according to the developments of the scenes and the depth of the emotions.

Regarding the novel's title, there is nothing more problematic than what the author said in one of his interviews:

> I think that the name came upon me, and I'm not even sure where it came from, nor why. I think it has something to do with the child-hood of the protagonist of the book, and the destructive fights his mother went through against the world of men. Maybe it's also partly because the book takes place in the '70s and the '80s: a generation that was engulfed by the dreams of liberality but chained by the need to control. I don't know why my characters lived those romantic, painful moments as they mix their love for their land with their love for their women. Maybe, it's because I truly appre-ciate the women of the rivers, who slapped the extremist men on the face and woke them up from their delusions. Maybe, finally on a deep personal level, it's an attempt by me to regain my own childhood and to bring my own sister, and my childhood friends, to the land of this earth. Maybe because I met the love of my life in a church in Damascus on the twenty-first of March, maybe for other reasons I'm not aware of.

Finally, let me quote the book:

The photo of Noura passes in my mind, I drown in the lake of her eyes, and she holds me closely. I hear her voice; it comforts me through the phone. She says she is happy now that she is back with her family; maybe she will finally settle down with Yousef in Cyprus, or they might return to Syria or Jordan. She asks me to take care of myself, and I say, laughing, "Thank you, Mum." I sit up in my chair, with tears in my eyes. I drown in the waterfall of her photos, walking barefoot on a beach, the waves kissing her toes, and escape shyly. She hits my chest with her hands, laughing, with tears in her eyes. I hold her hand, and she sleeps comfortably in my arms, drinking my wine. I wish I could kiss you in your sleep. She laughs at the shore of the sea. She hides the silver of the moonshine between her lips. I tell her: I almost died. She laughs, crying. She hits my chest. The tears fall upon her face, she slips away from the warmth of my hands; she sits calmly, surrendering: she is one with the moon and the sea.

9

A Male Escort for Every Female Scholar

. . .

WE READ A headline today in the newspapers; it was both a tragedy compared only with the plight of the poor and the sad, and a comedy to be faced only with sarcasm.

The Saudi Arabian Ministry of Higher Education has informed Saudi female scholars in the United Kingdom they have eight weeks to prove a male companion accompanies each of them.

The news carries with it two paradoxes:

First, the Ministry of Higher Education singled out the female scholars in the U.K., despite the thousands of female scholars in the many other countries around the world. This is a very dangerous indication that the fever of extremism has found its way into the minds of our female scholars in Britain.

Second, such a demand is a real and serious disparagement of the rights of women. It will cause embarrassment to all of them in front of their universities and public and civil organizations there.

To those in power in the ministry who released such a demand: Saudi female scholars include Dr. Adah al-Mutairi[16] and Dr. Hayat Sindi,[17] among thousands of creative minds who honor their nation in many fields. They should be honored, too. We should hold them in high regard.

Finally, Dr. So-and-so was banned from finishing her studies in the U.K., and she was shipped on the first airplane to Saudi Arabia when she couldn't come up with a male escort.

What a shame! What a shame!

10

The Day of the Nation

. . .

"THE WIDER THE views, the narrower the words."
A sentence that was said by al-Niffari, one of the
highly regarded Sufi clerics, who said it in Bagh-
dad centuries ago, back when the Arabian era was
flourishing. In my memory, which hasn't aged that
much yet, I hold this sentence clearly: it comes to
mind as we see the celebrations of our homeland,
Saudi Arabia, and its national day.

The concept of a nation is wide: it includes everyone under its love. The wider it gets, the more hatred
fills the hearts of some of our fellow citizens, adding
layers of sectarianism, tribalism, and narrow ways
of thinking. One of the most honorable bases for a
united nation is that it shouldn't be built upon the
specifics of one person, or one line of thought, or one
organization, or one group, excluding everyone else.

A homeland is for everyone, without marginal-
ization: a nation for its entire people, with all of their

beliefs and intellectual characteristics. Only through the establishment of this theory of one nation can everyone have the right to celebrate belonging to this land, to this geographical location, and to this soil.

That's why we Saudis have the right to celebrate a national day, because we're not only celebrating our nation but also celebrating ourselves, for ourselves.

When we celebrate a nation, we celebrate our rights as citizens of this nation. When we celebrate the day of this nation, we jump across those limited lines of narrow thinking. The bases of citizenship are clear: it's a victory for the variety of ideologies and a celebration of diversity, which leads us to the triumph of a civil society.

No one can deny us our right to celebrate this day, which is dear to all of us: we simply cannot allow a return to this Stone Age dogma, and we will fight it with all of our power. Such a celebration of the day of one nation is also a blow to those with their heads stuck in the Stone Age.

This day shows the importance and the necessity of a diverse civil structure in our nation that should embrace everyone, including those who stand as enemies to belonging to the soil and the geographical location. It should include them, even when they prefer their twisted ideology, an ideology that ruins the reputation of our nation, locally, regionally, and internationally.

"Nation" is a great word, and only those who truly love their nation know its true meaning and value. They see the nation as a holy, sacred place, more important than anything else. The nation will stay, as long as they protect it with their souls, money, and through the next generation.

Happy National Day, my dear homeland, and you too, people of my nation.

11

Mixed or Divided

. . .

MY PATERNAL GRANDMOTHER used to tell me stories about the simple honesty of a farmer's life: side by side, women farmers used to make decisions with their men. My southern grandmother explained to me that women used to participate in all aspects of life: work, celebrations, decision-making, among other things. Her tales proved to me that the village community was an open, civilized society, integrating everyone into its fabric.

She told me stories about the celebration of festivals: it wasn't long ago that women partook in a joyful folk dance known as "The Step" in a refined tradition to which no one at the time objected. Women used to cultivate the fields alongside men in their farms. They used to work in most crafts and businesses with men in the marketplaces. No one gave a second thought to this illusion of "gender mix" we created for ourselves thirty years ago.

I honestly wonder about the contradictions we have about rejecting gender mixing in the workplace now. On the one hand, surprisingly, many establishments in Jeddah welcome women in the workplace without a problem. Those establishments are located in high-class neighborhoods and in large malls, and women there are rarely bothered by anyone.

On the other hand, most small companies, located within what are known as the lower-class neighborhoods, do not allow women to work. If one of these companies dared to hire a woman, punishment and accountability would await both the woman and the workplace. This happens every day, despite the fact that no clear rule or ministerial decision was made to punish a company for hiring a woman alongside men.

At the same time, there is a law that allows women to work side by side with men in hospitals, where women step up and take their righteous place.

Why this contradiction? When will this matter be resolved, concluding its endless quest for an answer, as it roams the maze of the many different lines of thought?

There is a simple answer: a woman working in a public space is equal to a man; she needs the work just like a man. Sometimes her need for work is more urgent than his. When will we give up our misogynist, unfair ideals? When will we give up the many excuses supporting these ideals? Are we going to continue to fight the Saudi woman, who is only seeking her livelihood?

If we continue to limit women's lives, some might have to take immoral routes to bring bread to the table.

12

Let's Talk about Enlightenment

. . .

MANY OF THOSE who judge liberalism are ignorant about what it really means. They try to advertise liberalism as a line of thinking that rejects religion, somehow suggesting liberalism is a religion of its own. This cannot be further from the truth.

Many of these people are reluctant to accept anything modern. They loathe anything that gives humans their right to freedom. They fear this will pull the carpet from underneath the clerics, whose sole trade is in buying people's minds. They continue to promote liberalism as moral decay and degeneration.

Liberalism is subject to the judgment of the majority in the free societies, where all different ways of thinking are equal. Every intellectual has the right to promote and discuss his own philosophy. This gives the people the right to pick what they like from these views and methods.

The problem arises when the whole society is forced into one singular line of thinking and one simple philosophy under the ruling regime. This reigning viewpoint always works to distort the rest of the notions, announcing itself as the only path towards truth. This line of thinking trusts that everything it believes is the only shiny truth. It comes out saying it is the society's decision to reject liberalism. This is untrue. Let's allow everyone to stand on the same stage, and only then can we tell what the people really choose.

Liberalism is not connected to the attitude of one person: it's unfair to pick upon the ways of one person and consider him an example of everything liberal, when this person is anything but. Liberalism doesn't worship people, nor does it have a single authority; there is no one group of people who is considered a sample of what the liberal party is.

The reason for that is simple: when people change their views, liberalism doesn't fall apart as a concept; it doesn't stand on the shoulders of leaders or statues.

Let me summarize: liberalism means to simply live and let live. We should all acknowledge our respect for the traditions and personal behaviors of others, as long as they don't cross the line for others and invade their personal space. It's a natural human right to say what you want and do what you want, as long as this freedom is ruled by laws: your freedom ends on the outskirts of the freedom of others.

13

Is Liberalism Against Religion?

. . .

THIS QUESTION WAS the center of a fiasco of dis-
agreement in one of the public forums, based on
a series of articles I started to write about liberalism. Most of the attendees insisted liberalism, first
and foremost, is an enemy of all religions, especially
Islam, and considered it to be a religion of its own.

This is exactly where the debacle occurs—in the
superficial understanding of the concept of liberalism in our collective consciousness as a community
that was raised to believe in one opinion and one
religious sect. Liberalism is seen through this poi-
sonous filter that was placed upon the minds of our
society; it's seen as blasphemy, disbelief, immoral-
ity—naked beaches and gay marriage. Those are the
only ways people see the concept and practice of
liberalism.

A French writer describes liberalism, despite its
many meanings and the many developments it's

been through, as a simple curative idea: the human race is mature enough and capable of making its own decisions and deciding its own future without an external guardianship.

A political system that takes liberalism as its guidance is an optimistic regime that believes in the ability of human unity to establish advancement through dialogue and to learn from its mistakes by repeated experimentation.

Liberalism is based on the concept of personal freedom and respect for the freedoms of others. It's about mutual tolerance that is not ruled by indifference or disinterest.

The belief system of liberalism is advancement. It believes freedom in itself is good and works towards good. It believes the truth comes out of dialogue, and constant improvement is a natural movement for humanity.

Yes! Sensible and intelligent humanity is the sole catalyst and motivator for people to build societies, to lead in leniency and creativity, and to support the arts and technological developments.

Religion has no role to play in human civil advancement, which doesn't degrade any religion, simply because religions are about a very special and delicate spiritual relationship between a human and a creator.

The holy Quran is a great book for pure spiritual worship. As was said in the Quran: "Be pious scholars of the Lord because of what you have taught of the Scripture," and "That was a nation which has passed on. It will have [the consequence of] what it earned, and you will have what you have earned. And you will not be asked about what they used to do."

Man-made laws are an inescapable human and social need; traffic laws, workplace laws, and a government in all its aspects cannot be driven by religion.

Liberalism provides all that is necessary for individual freedoms, as well as freedom of religion, without imposing upon the society the tutelage of a certain sect or tyrant. Liberalism frees people from being forced to practice certain rituals. No one is pressured for personal gain; it becomes a shared attainment.

Those who reject it are the Islamists, the Western right wing, and the fusty Europeans of the medieval ages. They are those who stood in the face of the French Revolution and who stood by the Church and feudalism.

Religions, according to the concept of liberalism, are personal and special choices. A liberal country has no religion, which doesn't mean it's godless. It means it protects the rights of all the religions and nurtures all of them without distinction or upholding one over the others. It doesn't apple-polish the majority's religion over the minorities'.

Liberalism is based on knowledge and appreciation of a free and good life for all, and this view goes in harmony with religion: both always call for good, love, and peace.

14

The Book

• • •

FOR THE FIRST time in the history of Riyadh's International Book Fair, officials announced entry is now open to both genders on all days. The fair used to be segregated. This is a positive step for which we should thank the Ministry of Culture and Information.

With this advanced step, we should clarify the common misunderstanding between gender mixing and *khalwa* (meaning "nook"). You see, in the interest of preventing excuses, both expressions now mean the same thing, closing the door in the face of any diligence in such matters.

Let's start by explaining what "nook" really means according to sharia: it is the meeting of a man and a woman alone in a closed room, where no third person is present, and no one sees them. Think of it like a top-secret operation, unseen by the public, allowing the possibility for a forbidden act to take place between the two—and let me stress the concept of "possibility" here.

"Nook" is not actually forbidden in sharia and is not punishable in Islamic laws; the prophet, peace be upon him, said "If a man and a woman were alone in a nook, then the Devil is their third." The saying doesn't deny the two the right to join in one place, and it doesn't clearly state the Devil will win "nook-ing" people over to his evil side.

If attending places where devils gather is forbidden, then all of us should never go to public markets; it seems devils gather there, too.

Gender mixing is the gathering of women and men in public spaces: such as mosques, during the pilgrimage, in wars, in social events like weddings and the like, on public transportation, in schools and universities, in the workplace, etcetera. Mixing is not forbidden, and those who say so are slandering both the prophet and Allah: they basically forbid what Allah never ordered forbidden. The only way to forbid a human right should be through a clear Quranic verse, which is the pure devout ruling. No human has the right to forbid or grant what Allah stated otherwise. Allah says in his holy book: "And who is more unjust than he who invents a lie about Allah? Those will be presented before their Lord, and the witnesses will say, 'These are the ones who lied against their Lord.'"

There is plenty of evidence that mixing was allowed, especially during the life and times of the prophet, peace be upon him. Back in the time of the prophet, according to al-Bukhari's[18] *Book of Ablutions*, men and women cleansed themselves for prayer times together. Abdullah ibn Umar[19] also says men and women used to perform the ablutions together at the time of the prophet, peace be upon him. "We used to cleanse ourselves from the same bowl, we used to dip our hands together," says Abdullah ibn Umar.

Women also used to attend prayer times directly behind men, without any curtains dividing them the way it is now in the mosques of Allah. During prayers, women also used to uncover their faces. This is the exact opposite of what we're doing nowadays, when we force women to cover their faces in the holy mosques.

Gender mixing used to be a common practice in the time of the prophet, and the books about that time witness the participation of women in both political and social life, side by side with men.

We need to deny the voices of extremism; we need to turn a deaf ear to those who call for banning gender mixing not only at the book fair but also in many aspects of life. We need to provide a fair chance to all the sons and daughters of this country and clear away the rotten layer of religious terrorism and extremism that rises every now and then.

We need to wake up and get up to speed.

15

The Arab Spring between the Secular Choice and the Myth of Examples

. . .

I CAN SAY, WITH total conviction, that all the books published by the Rational Arab Association[20] are worth reading many times over. The books published by the association have proven without a doubt that it pays no attention to the quantity of books published but rather cares deeply for the depth of a book, its message, and the quality of the ideas it represents.

Among their books, let's take a minute to talk about *The Secular Choice and the Myth of Examples*, written by the famous Moroccan author Saeed Nasheed.[21] The book is published by the Rational Arab Association, in collaboration with al-Taliyah publishing house in Beirut. It's one of the very few books that forces you to read it multiple times, without a sense of boredom but rather with the eyes of a researcher and scholar. I'm not exaggerating when I say it really affected the way I view the Western secular example in its pure form and pushed me to an abyss of torturous rereads and deep research.

In his presentation of his book, the author gave a number of hypothetical questions: he asked himself if he has the right to point his pen and direct his critical thinking towards the secular hypocrisy of nations that are more civilized than his own nation. He also asked himself: Who am I to criticize nations that I'm supposed to be humbled by? And he considered examples for a future that we haven't reached yet. I can even add to what the author said by pointing out our current reality hasn't formed the structure of our own civilization; we are still living the primitive opposite of it, while we're at the doors of the third millennia.

Book critics usually ask such hypothetical questions. Here, and in a moment of pure genius, Nasheed managed to beat them to these questions, and he asked them in his book's introduction. His answers were screaming loudly across the rest of the book.

Nasheed is betting on the wills and minds of the Arab elite and youth, in hopes of forming an Arabian secular example that is brand-new and unlike any Western ideals. He wants that ideal to be a legitimate son coming from within his own nation. Nasheed uses bygone examples from those who built nations and made history on their own. He speaks about their struggles for a structure without ready-made examples. French revolutionaries, for example, weren't searching for an example to emulate in their revolution. If they did, they wouldn't have been able to create the great French republican example. Other examples are the founding fathers of the United States and the Russian Bolsheviks.

Finally, he honors the Arab Spring and the social and political revolutions that stormed the region and brought down the biggest and most ruthless dictatorship in our Arab world.

In reality, when a thinker says there is no solution in copying the secular Western example in its pure form, this thinker opens the doors of hell upon himself, regardless of who he is and how important he might be. He stands bare-chested, facing the firing squad of copycats and blind followers. Nasheed might be vulnerable in the eyes of those people, but he is clearly standing tall while pulling the map of a new road out of the neck of the bottle. He challenges the ready-made secular Western ideals.

"If they attempted to copy others, their creation would be either comic or weak, like the many who attempted the same before them," Nasheed says. "Such attempts are only remembered in the realm of news and warning lessons."

Every new creation at the time of its debate seems like a step away from reality, a dream of impossibility. New worlds, however, are never born without a break from the norm. The obsession with finding a ready-made example is similar to the need of a teenage boy for a father figure to give guidance. It's a clear sign this nation is still lacking in development and weak in its base.

Let's try to translate this into a clear political slogan: "A secular country is an orphan one." It has no father, neither from the realm of the unseen nor from the protection of every other example around it.

What else? A pure secular consciousness looks for no father other than secularism itself.

What else? To avoid confusion in these confusing times, we tell the clowns who present us with exciting scenes of self-criticism, aiming only to entertain or scare, that the Islamic example is dead; your self-criticism is like beating a dead horse.

This is a boring scene; let the curtains fall. Let's discuss the situation in the daylight. What about the Western example? Because of the current cultural atmosphere and the new economic situation, this supposed Western structure is threatening the future of democracy, the values of enlightenment, and the foundation of the French Revolution. It is starting to derail from the promises of the age of enlightenment towards the far right, religious, conservative goals that are somehow colonizing.

This Western example is based on the value of superiority and power; it relies completely on the servitude of poor nations to their external loans. It's based on the colonizing division and the support of some groups and some military forces in the regions of the East and South. It is based on the heritage of the

Cold War and the dozens of religious networks that were used as an antidote to the lure of Communism.

This Western example is heavy with the delusions of total control over the keys to wealth and the secrets of power. It is threatening the values that created the magic of the West over many decades: the values of intelligence, equality, world peace, protection of the environment, conviviality, and the many other values that will lead to the immortality of humanity.

It's starting to threaten the good lives of the citizens within the Western communities themselves.

It's threatening the unity of humanity.

It's threatening its own survival in a time when no Noah's ark is coming to the rescue.

Now, as you put down your own torture devices, you shouldn't let yourself go into the abyss of despair. Here are all my cards, unfolded: we haven't started yet; we will not start unless we realize we have to start not where the others finished, not upon what our ancestors built, but we have to start anew.

If Nasheed knew there would be many dramatic and radical geopolitical changes in the Middle East during the Arab Spring, he might have waited a bit before publishing his book. The Tunisians, Egyptians, Yemenis, Syrians, and Libyans are now living in reality the beginning he spoke of.

His only solace is that he was the only person who saw these revolutions coming, even in the papers of a book.

NOTES

•   •   •

1. A fatwa is a legal ruling from a Muslim authority that is bind-
    ing for those who recognize this authority.

2. At the time Badawi was writing his blog posts, Hamza Kash-
    gari was a columnist with the newspaper *Al-Bilad*. At the
    beginning of 2012, Kashgari became the target of Saudi inves-
    tigators on account of three tweets that were considered to be
    critical of Islam. Kashgari—who had in the meantime fled to
    Malaysia—was extradited to Saudi Arabia. He was imprisoned
    for almost two years, until the end of 2013. The tweets for
    which he was convicted were written on the occasion of the
    holiday of Mawlid an-Nabi (the prophet's birthday):

    *"On Your birthday, I will say that I love the revolutionary in You,
    who has always inspired me. But I do not like the halo. I do not pray
    to You."*

    *"On Your birthday, I see You wherever I look. I have loved certain
    aspects of You, hated others, and have not understood many."*

    *"On Your birthday, I will not bow down before You and I will not
    kiss Your hand. Instead, I will shake it as equals do, and I will
    smile at You while You smile at me. I will speak to you as a friend
    and not in any other way."*

3. Turki al-Hamad is a well-known Arabic writer and intellectual whose main work, the trilogy *Phantom of Deserted Alley*,
is one of a number of works forbidden in Saudi Arabia. Islamists have repeatedly called for the murder of al-Hamad.

4. Sheikh Mohammed bin Othman was, until his death on 2001,
one of the most influential Sunni spiritual leaders in the Arab
world and a leading cleric in Saudi Arabia.

5. Conservative Islamic scholars make a literal interpretation
of passages in the Quran that allude to physical events and
consider these passages to be irrefutably correct. Some of
their interpretations conflict with scientific knowledge. For
instance, the shape of the earth, which they claim is flat, the
design of heaven or the cosmos (heaven is arranged in multiple levels), or the orbits of the planets (the sun revolves around
the earth). To this day, Saudi sharia scholars, in particular,
claim that this world view is correct, and they accuse propo-
nents of scientific views that say otherwise of heresy.

6. One year after Badawi wrote this—in September 2011—an
Islamic cultural center was opened near ground zero.
Whether it was appropriate to open such a center at the site of
the Al-Qaeda attacks was hotly debated in the United States.

7. "God Is Great."

8. As part of this initiative, King Abdullah of Saudi Arabia
founded, among other institutions, the King Abdullah bin
Abdulazziz Center for Interreligious and Intercultural Dialogue, based in Vienna. In October 2011, the governments of
Austria, Spain, and Saudi Arabia signed a contract for the con-
struction of the center, which was opened in November 2012.

9. I.e., Islam, Christianity, and Judaism.

10. Hanbali is one of the four different schools of Sunni Islam. The orientation is conservative and has, among other things, a strong influence on Salafi thought, which is often open to criticism in Europe as well because of its strict interpretation of Islam.

11. A region in the Middle East. Cyprus, Egypt, Iraq, Israel, Jordan, Lebanon, Palestine, Syria, and Turkey are sometimes considered Levant countries.

12. Abdullah al-Qasemi was a Saudi intellectual who was very controversial in the Arab world. In his later work, he argued for radical secularization. He called into question the existence of God, whereupon his books were banned in the Arab world.

13. The January 25 Revolution is the name usually used in the Arab world to describe the 2011 Egyptian revolution that led to the fall of the long-standing dictator Hosni Mubarak. On January 25, 2011, as a result of the so-called Arab Spring, there was a series of demonstrations in Egypt, in particular in Tahrir Square. Millions of people participated, and under this pressure, the old regime announced it was stepping down.

14. Sheikh Imam was a famous Egyptian composer and singer. He came from impoverished circumstances and lost his sight when he was still a child. Later, he was jailed many times because of his anti-government songs.

15. If a woman has been divorced from her husband twice and remarries him each time, and if he then divorces her a third time, under Islamic law he is not allowed to marry her again. That is haram, that is to say, forbidden. To deal with this problem, a different form of marriage was created. Officially known as "the borrowed ram," this practice is said to go back to the prophet himself. The borrowed ram is a man who

marries a woman for the night and then divorces her. After she has had a marriage with another man, it is once again lawful for her to return to her previous husband. The term "borrowed ram" comes from the practice of goat herders occasionally borrowing a ram to inseminate their female goats. Moreover, the ram is said to have a strong sexual drive.

16. Adah al-Mutairi is a professor who specializes in biology and medicine. She is the director of the Center for Excellence of Nanomedicine at the University of California San Diego in the United States.

17. Hayat Sindi is a medical scientist who specializes in biotechnology.

18. Sahih al-Bukhari is the name of a collection of hadiths, that is to say, sayings and teachings of the prophet Mohammed.

19. Abdullah ibn Umar was a prominent authority on hadiths and law.

20. Established in Paris in 2007.

21. Saeed Nasheed is a well-known Moroccan intellectual, who got deeply involved in discussions about the origins of the Arab Spring.

ORIGINAL PUBLICATIONS

· · ·

1. **Religious Vocation Entraps the Freedom of the Arab Thinker**

   Al-Hewar al-Mutamaddin, August 12, 2010

2. **Defaming the Intellectuals and the Inquisition Courts: Turki al-Hamad as an Example**

   Al-Hewar al-Mutamaddin, February 18, 2012

3. **Let's Lash Some Astronomers**

   Al-Bilad, September 7, 2011

4. **No to Building a Mosque in New York City**

   Al-Hewar al-Mutamaddin, September 13, 2010

5. **Yes! I Will Fight Theists and Religious Thoughts**

   Al-Hewar al-Mutamaddin, November 15, 2010

6. **Tahrir Square Brought Students Back to Hard Work**

   Al-Hewar al-Mutamaddin, February 11, 2011

7. **The Traveler's Marriage and the Borrowed Ram**

   Al-Bilad, January 8, 2012

8. **The Kingdom Come of the Syrian Spring**
    Al-Hewar al-Mutamaddin, January 5, 2012

9. **A Male Escort for Every Female Scholar**
    Al-Bilad, December 12, 2011

10. **The Day of the Nation**
    Al-Bilad, September 9, 2011

11. **Mixed or Divided**
    Al-Bilad, September 10, 2011

12. **Let's Talk About Enlightenment**
    Al Jazeera, April 2012

13. **Is Liberalism Against Religion?**
    Al Jazeera, May 2012

14. **The Book**
    Al Jazeera, no date available

15. **The Arab Spring between the Secular Choice and the Myth of Examples**
    Al Jazeera, no date available

BIOGRAPHIES

. . .

RAIF MUHAMMAD BADAWI is a Saudi Arabian writer who in 2008 founded the online forum Free Saudi Liberals, a website about politics and religion. He has been imprisoned in Jeddah, Saudi Arabia, since 2012.

CONSTANTIN SCHREIBER is a lawyer and journalist who has lived and worked for many years in the Middle East and is fluent in Arabic. He is currently a news anchor for the German network n-tv and a presenter in Arabic for the Egyptian channel ONTV in Cairo.

LAWRENCE M. KRAUSS is director of the Origins Project at Arizona State University and foundation professor in the School of Earth and Space Exploration and the Physics Department at ASU. He is a best-selling author of many books, including *The Physics of* Star *Trek* and *A Universe from Nothing,* and is a vocal advocate of the importance of science and reason as opposed to religion and superstition.

AHMED DANNY RAMADAN is a journalist with bylines appearing in the *Washington Post*, the *Guardian*, and *Foreign Policy* for his reporting in the Middle East. He is also a translator and author, with two collections of short stories published in Arabic.